Florence Nightingale
and the Crimean War

Jane Shuter

Heinemann
LIBRARY

www.heinemann.co.uk/library

Visit our website to find out more information about **Heinemann Library** books.

To order:

 Phone 44 (0) 1865 888066

 Send a fax to 44 (0) 1865 314091

💻 Visit the Heinemann Bookshop at www.heinemann.co.uk/library to browse our catalogue and order online.

First published in Great Britain by Heinemann Library, Halley Court, Jordan Hill, Oxford OX2 8EJ, part of Harcourt Education.
Heinemann is a registered trademark of Harcourt Education Ltd.

Editorial: Lucy Thunder and Helen Cox
Design: David Poole and Geoff Ward
Illustrations: Debbie Boon at Eikon Illustration
Picture Research: Hannah Taylor
Production: Séverine Ribierre

Originated by Repro Multi Warna
Printed and bound in Hong Kong, China by South China Printing

ISBN 0 431 12345 4
07 06 05 04 03
10 9 8 7 6 5 4 3 2 1

British Library Cataloguing in Publication Data

Shuter, Jane
How do we know about Florence Nightingale and the Crimean War?
610.7'3'092
A full catalogue record for this book is available from the British Library.

Acknowledgements

The publishers would like to thank the following for permission to reproduce photographs: Antiquarian Images p**4**; Florence Nightingale Museum pp**5**, **18**, **22**, **24**, **26**; John and Hilary Malcolm p**23**; John Frost Newspapers p**19**; National Army Museum pp**20**, **25**; National Portrait Gallery p**21**; Tudor Photography p**27**.

Cover photograph of Florence nursing the sick, reproduced with permission of Corbis.

The publishers would like to thank Rebecca Vickers for her assistance in the preparation of this book.

Every effort has been made to contact copyright holders of any material reproduced in this book. Any omissions will be rectified in subsequent printings if notice is given to the publishers.

Contents

Any words shown in the text in bold, **like this**, are explained in the Glossary.

A woman at war

Crimea

In 1854, Turkey and Russia were fighting a war in a part of Russia called the **Crimea**. Britain joined the war to fight on Turkey's side.

One of the most famous people to go to the Crimea was a young woman called Florence Nightingale. She wanted to help the soldiers **wounded** in the war.

Learning to nurse

Florence Nightingale was born in 1820. In those days, girls from rich families did not work. Florence wanted to train as a nurse, but her parents said no.

So Florence visited **nurse training schools** in Europe to find out more. There were no schools for nurses in England.

Danger and disease

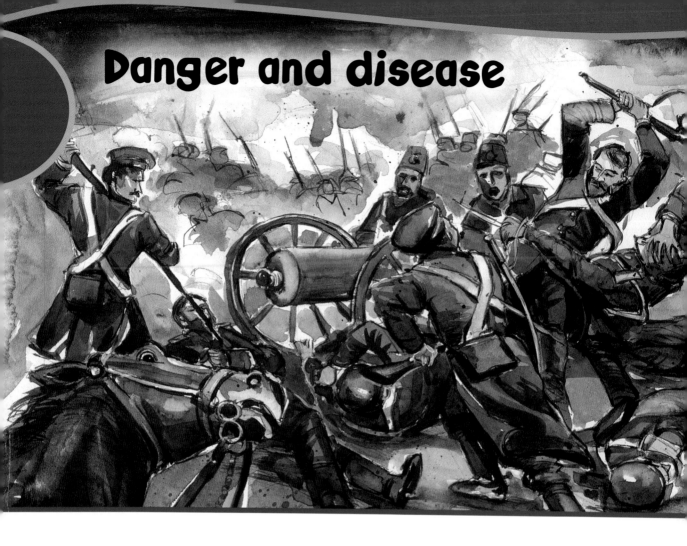

In 1854, ships took British soldiers to
fight in the **Crimea**. The ships also
carried horses, food, weapons, doctors,
medicine and tents.

Many soldiers were **wounded** in battle. Living so close together meant that diseases spread, too. The hospitals needed more doctors and medicine.

Shocking news

A **reporter** called William Russell wrote about the terrible hospitals in the **Crimea**. People at home were shocked. Sidney Herbert, a man in the **government**, asked Florence for help.

Florence chose 38 nurses to go with her to the Crimea. They travelled by train, then by ship to Scutari, in Turkey. Storms made their journey rough.

Making it better

When Florence and her nurses reached the hospitals in Scutari, they were not welcomed. Some people thought women should keep away from war.

Florence and her team scrubbed the
wards clean and changed the dirty
bed-sheets. Far more **wounded**
soldiers stayed alive while in their care.

Ways of caring

The nurses cared for the **wounded** soldiers in many different ways. They wrote letters to their families at home, mended their clothes and read to them.

Florence was known as 'the lady with the lamp', as she checked her patients every night. Although ill, she stayed in Scutari until the war ended in 1856.

Britain's heroine

When Florence came home, she became a **heroine**. People collected money to help her start a **nurse training school** in England. She wrote a book about nursing, too.

Florence's health never really got better from her time in Scutari. But she still worked to improve hospitals and medical care. She died in 1910.

How do we know?

Scutari

Maps show us where the **Crimea** is, and where the war was fought. This map from the time shows Scutari, in Turkey, where Florence and her nurses worked.

THE CRIMEA.

[A portion of the following appeared in our second edition of yesterday :—]

(FROM OUR OWN CORRESPONDENT.)

THE FLEET, OFF THE RIVER KATCHA, CRIMEA, SEPT. 26.

This morning the whole steam squadron, with the Agamemnon at the head of it, and accompanied by several transports carrying siege guns, steamed off at 7 o'clock, with the intention, it is said, of co-operating with the army, which is expected to reach the creek of Balaklava in the course of the day. The crews of the huge line-of-battle ships looked after the steaming squadron with a heavy heart, seeing vanish with it their hopes of glory and prize money. Especially since the battle of the Alma, which the fleet, sailing close to land, could witness very well, a wish to emulate the heroism of the land troops, has seized hold of the crews, and not all the horrors which the fatigue parties sent on shore the next day to help in transporting the wounded saw on the field of battle have cooled their ardour. Two days ago the rumour was spread in the Agamemnon that Sir Edmund Lyons, the idol of the fleet, was to go in the Highflyer to undertake something against Sebastopol. The crew sent a deputation, requesting the Admiral not to forget the Agamemnon ; as they had borne all the trouble and fatigue, they wished also to have some of the fun. Sir Edmund is said to have assured them that they should go wherever he went, and the Agamemnon could go. This is not a little to say, for the Agamemnon goes about in places where certainly no line-of-battle ship ever thought of going before. Sir Edmund Lyons's brougham, as it is sometimes called, is not at all a bad name for her.

OFF BALAKLAVA, SEPT. 28.

Early yesterday morning the transport steamers, taking in tow the vessels containing siege implements, began to go down in the direction of Balaklava. The Agamemnon came up to the entrance

Russians that the attack would be from the north obviously suggested an attack on a point which might be found less prepared. The Russians had surrounded Fort Constantine with a triple rampart, while the town itself is merely encircled with a wall, which may be battered down from a distance of about 800 yards, and the place then taken by assault.

The admiration excited by the zeal and readiness of Admiral Lyons is very great both in the army and fleet. Every one speaks of the skill and perseverance with which all the plans for the disembarcation and supply of the troops have been carried out. The personal activity of the Admiral, who shoots about in the Agamemnon wherever his presence may be required, is not the least important of his valuable qualities.

While the navy receives its due reward, not only for its own independent exploits, but for the way in which it co-operates with the army, and prepares the way for victories in which it does not share, it perhaps is not well quite to forget the humbler but still most useful and arduous duties performed by the transport service, and particularly by the officers and crews of those gigantic steamers the employment of which on a large scale for the conveyance of troops is one of the most striking features of this expedition. The labour of a zealous officer commanding one of these large ships is almost incessant, and has been lately of a kind more disagreeable and depressing than any encountered by their highly placed brethren of the Queen's service. It is true that some ships have been neglected, and are soon allowed to become a perfect stye of filth and disorder, much to the disadvantage of the troops conveyed, who have in more than one case received the seeds of fever and cholera amid the dirt and bad smells of the outward voyage. But in general the regiments have been conveyed to the East and from one station to another in great comfort, but at a cost of labour which should not remain unnoticed, nor be supposed quite re-

unless some friend happen to see one by chance in the Post-office, and sends it back by a private hand. Consequently, the private soldiers never get their letters at all. There are officers here who have not heard from their relations in England for five weeks, although they know that several letters have been sent to them during that time. The French have a number of active men called "Administrateurs de la Poste d'Orient," and letters are duly sent back to invalids by the simple plan of registering every man's name who leaves, and making up a bag for the return mail. At such a time these shortcomings are doubly deplorable, for the anxiety and suspense of families must be greater than at any former period. The common soldiers feel the neglect deeply, for they are always anxious to hear from home, and would often prefer a letter to a dinner.

MARSEILLES, OCT. 9.

The mail steamer Sinai, which sailed from Constantinople on the 30th ult, arrived here yesterday morning. Captain de Sardi, the commander, announces that shortly before his departure from Constantinople the Banshee and Ajaccio had arrived there from the coast of the Crimea, which they left on the 28th. The allied armies had begun to invest Sebastopol. It was expected that the regular siege would commence in form on the 30th, and that the town could not hold out many days, as the allies had 120 pieces of siege artillery to bring against it.

The two superior Russian officers captured are Generals Tchetchanoff and Gonikoff. They were dressed as simple privates, and were so treated until their rank was made known by their fellow-prisoners. They state the Russian force engaged as 35,000 men, but add that they considered that number quite sufficient to defend the position against the allied armies for five months.

The accounts from Varna are of the 27th ult. The army of reserve was embarked there on the 26th on board the French ships of the line Vill

Newspaper **articles** from the time have also survived. In this one, in *The Times*, the **reporter** William Russell describes the fighting in the Crimea.

Photos and paintings

Photographers took pictures of places and people in the Crimea, but not battles in action. It took fifteen minutes to take a photograph.

Artists painted pictures of the war, too.
Some used what people had said or
written to guide them. Others used
their imagination. This painting shows
Florence in a Scutari hospital.

A museum for Florence

The Florence Nightingale Museum in London has many things that belonged to Florence. This is the **slate** she wrote on when she was a child.

MISS
NIGHTINGALE

Florence's work made her so famous that people even made ornaments of her nursing the sick. This one shows Florence with a **wounded** soldier.

Survivors of war

Several **museums** have **artefacts** from the **Crimean** War. This is the **medicine chest** that Florence used in the hospital at Scutari.

Some soldiers' uniforms have survived from the war. The cloth the uniforms were made of did not give much **protection** from bullets, swords or knives.

Books

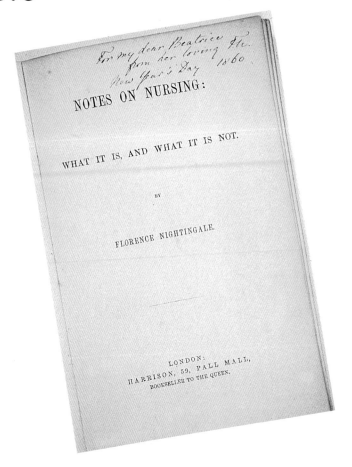

NOTES ON NURSING:

WHAT IT IS, AND WHAT IT IS NOT.

BY

FLORENCE NIGHTINGALE.

LONDON:
HARRISON, 59, PALL MALL,
BOOKSELLER TO THE QUEEN.

Florence wanted cleaner hospitals and training for nurses. Her aim was to teach people better **hygiene**. This is a copy of her book about this called *Notes on Nursing*.

People are still interested in finding out about Florence and the **Crimean** War. Many books have been written about the war and her nursing work.

Timeline

12 May 1820 Florence Nightingale is born.

June 1851 Florence starts three months' nurse training in Kaiserswerth, Germany.

October 1853 War between Turkey and Russia begins.

March 1854 Britain and France join the war between Turkey and Russia. Both help Turkey. Soon the fighting is mainly in the Crimea, so the war is known as the Crimean War.

21 October 1854 Florence Nightingale and her nurses leave for the hospitals at Scutari. They travel by train to Marseilles, in France, then by ship to Scutari.

3 November 1854 Florence Nightingale and her nurses arrive in Scutari.

30 March 1856 A **peace treaty** is signed to end the Crimean War. Soldiers allowed to go home.

29 April 1856 Fighting ends in the Crimean War.

December 1859 Florence's book *Notes on Nursing* is published.

May 1860 First students begin training at the Nightingale Training School in England.

13 August 1910 Florence Nightingale dies.

Biographies

Sidney Herbert

Sidney Herbert was born in 1810. He became a **politician**. From 1852 to 1855 he was Secretary of War in the **government**. He was responsible for getting soldiers and the things they needed to the Crimean War. He did not organize the fighting. It was Sidney who asked Florence Nightingale to go to the Crimea. After the Crimean War, Sidney worked to make changes in the army, including standards of **hygiene** and medical care. Florence helped him to plan these changes. Sidney died in 1861.

William Russell

William Russell was born in Ireland in 1820. He became a **reporter** for *The Times* newspaper in 1840. He wrote about the war in the Crimea and how the soldiers did not have proper food or even weapons to fight with. After the war, William gave talks about his time in the Crimea. When he stopped working for *The Times* in 1871, he travelled all over the world and wrote books and **articles** about what he saw. He died in 1907.

Glossary

artefact objects that are made by people

article report written for a newspaper or magazine by a reporter

Crimea now an area of land which is part of the Ukraine. It sticks out into the north end of the Black Sea.

government people who run a country

heroine a woman who has done something very brave and difficult

hygiene keeping things clean to stop the spread of germs which make people ill

medicine chest special box with places for medicines, ointments, bandages, needles and other things a nurse or doctor needs

museum building that has things in it that tell us about the past

nurse training school special school that teaches nurses how to look after people

peace treaty written document that is signed by countries when they are ready to end the war between them

politician person who works, or wants to work, in the government

protection looking after something and keeping it safe from harm

reporter person who finds out what is going on and then writes about it for a newspaper

slate piece of flat grey stone. Pieces of slate were used to teach children to write. They wrote on them with chalk, which was wiped off. Slates were used many times over.

wards rooms in hospitals where sick people are kept and cared for

wounded suffering from injuries

Further reading

Lives and Times: Florence Nightingale, Rebecca Vickers, Heinemann Library, 2001

Profiles: Florence Nightingale, Hamish Hamilton, 1987

Great Lives: Florence Nightingale, Wayland, 1988

Index

Titles in the *How Do we Know About ...?* series include:

Hardback   0 431 12344 6

Hardback   0 431 12346 2

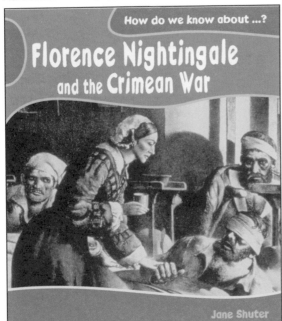

Hardback   0 431 12345 4

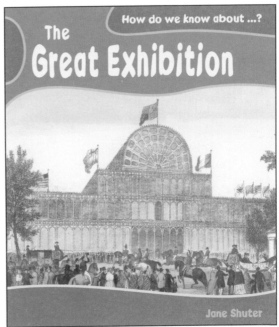

Hardback   0 431 12347 0

Find out about the other titles in this series on our website www.heinemann.co.uk/library